Japanese

Learn Japanese ex
travel to japan – Meet People , Socialize & Find Your Way around

Table of Contents

Copyright

Introduction

I want to thank you and congratulate you for downloading the book, *"Learn Japanese : In Only 1 Week! The Ultimate Course to Learning the Basic of Japanese in a Time Record"*

This book will help you master the basics of the Japanese language.

Each day, you will learn basic conversations using Japanese in different situations. You should be confident enough by the end of the week.

Thanks again for downloading this book, I hope you enjoy it!

Chapter 1 – Overview of the Japanese Language Structure

Although learning how to write in Japanese (katakana and hiragana) is very challenging, learning to speak the language is actually very easy. You just need to learn the basic Japanese language structure as well as basic words and you should be good to go.

Pronunciation

The Japanese language is easy to pronounce. The syllables are joined together following simple pronunciation rules. The syllables a, na, ta, for example are simply joined and pronounced *a-na-ta*, with each syllable having equal stress. The combinations of vowels (a-i, e-i, etc.) don't result in completely new sounds, unlike in English.

Consonants

Most of the consonants are pronounced in a normal manner like in English

b as in boy	b	bin	*bin*
ch as in chat	ch	niche	*ni-chi*
d as in dog	d	dame	*da-me*
f as in fast	f	fuyu	*fu-yu*
g as in goat	g	gogo	*go-go*
h as in hat	h	haru	*ha-ru*
j as in jaguar	j	niji	*ni-ji*
k as in koala	k	koko	*ko-ko*

m as in mother	m	totemo	*to-te-mo*
n as in nut	n	namae	*na-ma-e*
n may sound like ng as in king when at the end of a word			
p as in pot	p	posuto	*po-su-to*
r more like r in car	r	raigetsu	righ-gets
s as in sun	s	semete	semetay
sh as in shape	sh	shio	shi-o
t as in tap	t	doshite	doh-shtay
ts as in cats	ts	itsu	its
w as in wash	w	wakaru	wakaru
y as in yam	y	yoru	yoru
z as in zoo	z	mizu	mizu

Chapter 2 – Day 1: Basic Japanese Conversations

Personal details

In Japanese, the surname is mentioned first and then the given name. The title (-*san* for male and female adults and –*chan* for small children). Superiors also sometime call their subordinates with the surname plus –*kun*. An intellectual, like a teacher is called sensei (*sen-say*).

My name	*nama-e*
Your name	*onama-e*
Given name	*nama-e*
Surname	*say/myohji*
Sex (male/female)	*say (dan/jo)*
Date of birth	*say-nen-gappi*
Place of birth	*shushoh-chi*
Nationality	*koku-seki*
Single/married/divorced	*mi-kon/ki-kon/ri-kon*

Number of children *ko-domo (no kazu)*

Day and Date

What is the day today?	*Kyoh-wa nan-yohbi des-ka*
Today is Monday	*Kyoh-wa gets-yohbi des*
Today is Tuesday	*Kyoh-wa ka-yohbi des*
Today is Wednesday	*Kyoh-wa swee-yohbi des*
Today is Thursday	*Kyoh-wa moku-yohbi des*
Today is Friday	*Kyoh-wa kin-yohbi des*
Today is Saturday	*Kyoh-wa do-yohbi des*
Today is Sunday	*Kyoh-wa nichi-yohbi des*
In January	*ichi-gatsu-ni*
Since February	*ni-gatsu-kara*
In spring	*haru-ni*
In summer	*natsu-ni*
In autumn	*aki-ni*
In winter	*fuyu-ni*
2012	*n-sen joo-ni nen*
The twentieth century	*nijoo-say-ki*
The twenty-first century	*nijoo-is-say-ki*
What is the date today?	*Kyoh-wa nan-gatsu nan-nichi des-ka*
Today is the 24th	*Kyoh-wa nijoo-yokka des*

Monday 3 November 2012	*Ni-sen joo-ni nen joo-ichi-gatsu mikka gets-yohbi*
This week	*kon-shoo*
Next month	*righ-gets*
Last year	*kyo-nen*
Next ...	*...tsugi-no*
In ... days	*...nichi*
In ... weeks	*...shookan*
In ... months	*...ka-getsu*
In ... years	*...nenkan-ni*
... weeks ago	*...shookan ma-e-ni*
Day off	*kyoo-jitsu*

Time

In the morning	*asa-ni*
In the afternoon	*gogo-ni*
In the evening	*yoogata-ni*
At night	*yoru-ni*
This morning	*kesa*
This afternoon	*kyoh no gogo*
This evening	*kyoh no yoogata*
Tonight	*kom-ban*
Last night	*saku-ban*
What time is it?	*Ima nanji des-ka*

It's nine o'clock	*(gozen) ku-ji des*
-five past ten	*(gozen) joo-ji go-fun...*
-a quarter past eleven	*(gozen) joo-ichi-ji joo-go-fun...*
-twenty past twelve	*(gogo) joo-ni-ji ni-juppun...*
-half past one	*(gogo) ichi-ji han...*
-a quarter to four	*san-ji yon-joo-go-fun...*
-twenty-five to three	*ni-ji san-joo-go-fun...*
– twelve noon	*joo-ni-ji/shoh-go...*
– ten to five	*yo-ji go-juppun...*
–midnight	*yo-naka no joo-ni-ji...*
Half an hour	*san-juppun-kan*
What time?	*Nanji*
What time can I come by	*Nanji-ni kureba ee des-ka?*
After...	*...sugi-ni*
At...	*...ni*
Between...and...	*...to...no ai-da-ni...*
Before...	*...ma-e-ni*
In...minutes	*...fun go-ni*
From...to...	*...kara...maday*
In an hour	*...ichijikan go-ni*
-a quarter of an hour	*joo-go-fun go-ni*
-...hours	*..jikan go-ni*
-three quarters of an hour	*yon-joo-go-fun go-ni*

On time	*mani-attay*
Early	*haya-sugi-mas*
Late	*oso-sugi-mas*
I am sorry I am late	*Okurete sumi masen*
I will be a little bit late	*Sukoshi okure mas*

Numbers

Numbers in Japanese are usually joined with counters and are rarely used on their own. Here are some of the more common counters:

jikan (is used to count hours): *ichi-jikan* (1 hour), *san-jikan* (3 hours)

ji (is used for time): *ichi-ji* (1 o'clock), *san-ji* (3 o'clock)

yen (the currency in Japan): *hyaku-yen* (100 yen), *seng-yen* (1000 yen)

mai (is used for flat things like sheets of paper): *ichi-mai,*

san-mai, etc.

hon (is used for cylindrical things, like cigarettes, chopsticks,

etc.): *ip-pon, ni-hon, sam-bon*

hai (used for cups): *koh-hee ni-hai* (two cups of coffee), *o-cha san-hai* (three cups of tea)

dai (used for machines like bikes and cars): *ichi-dai, san-dai,* etc.

nin (is used for people): *san-nin* (three people), *go-nin* (five people).

If you are referring to one or two persons: *hi-to-ri* (one

person) and *fu-ta-ri* (two people).

0 (Zero) – Zero

1 – *Ichi*

2 – *Ni*

3 – *San*

4 – *Yon*

5 – *Go*

6 – *Roku*

7 – *Nana*

8 – *Hachi*

9 – *Kyuu*

10 – *Juu*

Once you go beyond 10, just combine the word *'juu'* with the preceding number. So 11 would be *juu ichi*, 12 will be *juu ni*, 13 would be *juu san*, and so forth until you reach 19.

20 will be the combination of the Japanese for 2 and for 10 so that would be *ni juu*. To proceed you add the preceding number to *nii juu*. So 21 would be *ni juu ichi*, 22 would be *ni juu ni*, 23 would be *ni juu san*, and so forth. The same principles apply to numbers up to 99. So 30 would be *san juu*, 40 would be *yon juu*, 91 would be *kyuu juu ichi*, and so forth until 99.

100 translates to *hyaku*, 1000 to *sen*, and 1 million to *hyaku man*. Combine this with the previous principles to express a particular number correctly in Japanese.

When referring to position like 1st, 2nd , or 3rd, just put the word *dai* before the number. So 1st would be *dai-ichi*, 2nd would be dai-ni, 3rd would be *dai-san*, and so forth.

When referring to frequency like once, twice, and thrice, just put the word *bai* after the number. So once would be *ichi-bai*, twice would be *ni-bai*, thrice would be *san-bai.*

Half	*han-bun*
Quarter	*yon-bun no ichi*
A third	*sam-bun no ichi*

In simple mathematics, plus is *tas*, minus is *hiku*, multiply by is *kakeru*, and divide by is *waru*. Equals is *wa*. So:

$4 - 2 = 2$	*yon hiku ni wa ni*
$2 + 4 = 6$	*ni tas yon wa roku*
$4 \div 2 = 2$	*yon waru ni wa ni*
2 x 4 = 8	*ni kakeru yon wa hachi*

Odd	*gu-su-no*
Even	*ki-su-no*
Total	*zem-bu*

Here and there

here	*koko*
there	*soko*
nowhere	*doko ni mo...nai*
somewhere	*doko-ka*
everywhere	*doko ni demo*
near	*chi-kigh*

far	*toh-i*
right	*migi no hoh ni*
left	*hidari no hoh ni*
to the right of...	*...no migi ni*
to the left of...	*...no hidari ni*
straight ahead	*mas-sugu*
via...	*...kay-yu de*
on...	*...no u-e ni*
in...	*...no naka ni*
under...	*...no shta ni*
opposite...	*...no mukoh-gawa ni*
against...	*...ni tigh-shtay*
near...	*...no soba ni*
next to...	*...no tonari ni*
in the center...	*...no man-naka ni*
in front of...	*...no ma-e ni*
forward	*ma-e ay*
up	*u-e ay*
down	*shta ay*
outside	*soto ay*
inside	*naka ay*
at the front	*ma-e ni*
behind	*ushiro ay*

at the back	*ushiro ni*
to the south	*minami no hoh ni*
in the north	*kita no hoh ni*
from the east	*hi-gashi no hoh kara*
from the west	*nishi no hoh kara*

Chapter 3 – Day 2: Meet and Greet

Courtesy is of utmost importance in Japan. Saying the phrase 'dohmo sumimasen' ('Thank you for your trouble.') is very much appreciated if someone does something for you. You may notice locals bowing to each other as a form of greeting or respect, though this custom is not expected from foreigners.

Remember to take your shoes off when you enter private homes. Japanese people have greater tolerance with regard to private space especially in public transportation and other crowded places.

Common greetings

Good morning	*O-high-yoh (goza-i-masu)*
Good evening	*Kom-ban wa*
Good afternoon /Hello	*Kon-nichi wa*
Good night	*Oyasumi nasa-i*
Good bye	*Sayo-nara*
How are you?	*O-genki des-ka*
Fine, thank you, and you?	*Hai, genki des. anata wa*
Not too bad	*Mah mah des*
Very well	*O-kagay-sama day*
I have to be going.	*Shto-o matasetay imas no*
I'd better be going	*Jah, shi-tsu-ray shimas*
Someone's waiting for me *itashimas*	*koray-de shi-tsu-ray*

See you soon	*Mata ato-day*
Have fun	*Tano-shinday kuda-sigh*
Good luck	*Gambattay kuda-sigh*
Have a good trip	*Tanoshee ryokoh-o*
Have a nice vacation	*Tanoshee kyookay-o*
Thank you, you too	*Dohmo arigatoh, anata-mo*
Say hello to...for me	*...ni yoroshku*

Asking questions

Who?	*Dare*
Who's that?	*Dare des-ka*
What?	*Nani*
What kind of hotel is that?	*Donna hoteru des-ka*
What's there to see here?	*Kono chikaku day nani-ka omoshiroi koto-ga arimas-ka*
Where?	*Doko*
Where are you going?	*Dochira-ni ikaremas-ka*
Where are you from?	*Doko-kara kimashta-ka*
Where's the bathroom?	*Toiray-wa doko-ni arimas-ka*
How?	*Doh*
How long does that take?	*Nan-jikan kakarimas-ka*
How far is that?	*Dono kurigh toh-i des-ka*

How long is the trip? *Ryokoh-wa dono kurigh kakarimas-ka*

How many? *Ikutsu des-ka*

How much? *Ikura des-ka*

How much is this? *Koray-wa ikura des-ka*

Which....? *Dono...*

Which? *Dore*

Which one is it? *Sono hitotsu wa, sore o aru*

When? *Itsu*

When are you leaving? *Itsu demas-ka*

Why? *Naze*

Why are you going? *Naze anata wa iku*

Why are we here? *Naze watashitachi wa koko ni iru?*

Could you help me, please? *Tetsudattay kudasa-i-masen-ka*

Could you point that out to me? *Oshietay kudasa-i-masen-ka*

Could you come with me, please? *Tsuretay ittay kudasa-i-masen-ka*

Do you know...? *...(o) shtte imas-ka*

Do you know another hotel? *Hoka-no hoteru-o shohkaigh shtay*

Do you have a...? *...(ga) arimas-ka*

Do you have a vegetarian dish, please? *Bejitarian-ryohri-wa arimas-ka?*

I'd like... *...onega-i-shimas*

I'd like a kilo of apples, please?	*Ringo-o ikkiro kuda-sigh*
Can I take this?	*Kore-o mottay ittay-mo ee des-ka*
Could I ask you something?	*Sumimasen-nga*
Can I smoke here?	*Tabako-o suttay-mo ee des-ka*

Replying to questions

Yes, of course	*Hai, mochiron*
No, I'm sorry	*I-ye, sumimasen*
Yes, what can I do for you?	*Hai, dohzo*
Just a moment, please	*Chotto matte kudasa-i*
No, I don't have time now	*Sumimasen-nga, jikan-nga arimasen*
No, that's impossible	*Fukanoh des*
I think so	*Soh omo-imas*
No, no one	*Dare-mo imasen*
No, nothing	*Nan demo arimasen*
It's okay	*Die-joh-bu des*
That's right	*Soray-day kekkoh des*
That's different	*Chiga-i-masu*
I agree	*Sansay des*
I don't agree	*Sansay dekimasen*
All right	*Ee es*
Okay	*Ee des-yo*

Perhaps	*Tabun*
I don't know	*Wakarimasen/shirimasen*

Appreciation

Thank you	*(dohmo) arigatoh*
You're welcome	*Doh itashi-mashtay*
Thank you very much	*Dohmo arigatoh goza-i-mas*
Very kind of you	*Go-shinsetsu-ni*
I enjoyed it very much	*Hontoh-ni tanoshikatta des*
Thank you for your trouble	*Dohmo arigatoh goza-i-mashta*
You shouldn't have	*Sumimasen deshta*
That's all right	*Doh itashimashtay*

Apologizing

Excuse me	*Sumimasen*
I'm sorry, I didn't know...	*...Shiranakatta no-day, mohshiwakay-arimasen*
I do apologize	*Sumimasen deshta*
I'm sorry	*Mohshi-wakay-arimasen*
I didn't do it on purpose, it was an accident	*Waza-to yatta wakay de-wa-nai no-day, oyurushi-kuda-sigh*
That's all right	*Ee des-yo*
Never mind	*Mah mah*

It could've happened to anyone	*Soray-wa daray-ni demo okori-eru des*

Speaking your mind

Which do you prefer?	*Dochira-ga o-ski des-ka*
What do you think?	*Doh omoimas-ka*
Don't you like dancing?	*Odoru no-ga ki-righ es-ka*
I don't mind	*Nandemo ee des*
Well done!	*Yokatta*
Not bad!	*Waruku-nai des-ne*
Great!	*Subarashee*
Wonderful food!	*Oi-shee*
It's really nice here!	*Tanoshee des-ne*
How nice!	*Steki*
How pretty!	*Kiray*
How nice for you!	*Ee des-ne*
I'm very happy with...	*...ni manzoku shitay imas*
I'm not very happy with ...	*...ni manzoku shitay imasen*
I'm glad...	*...ureshee*
I'm having a great time	*Totemo tanoshinde imas*
I'm looking forward to it	*Soray-o tanoshimi-ni mattay-imas*
That's great	*Sugoi*
What a pity!	*Zannen*

That's ridiculous!	*Baka-baka-shee*
What nonsense/How silly!	*Bakara-shee*
I don't like...	*...wa ki-righ des*
I'm bored to death	*Unzari da-yo*
I've had enough	*Moh akita*
This is no good	*Damay (da) yo*

Chapter 4 – Day 3: Small Chat

Introducing yourself and others

May I introduce myself?	*Jiko shohkigh shtay-mo yoroshee des-ka*
My name's…	*Watashi-wa…des*
What's your name?	*Onama-e-wa*
May I introduce…?	*Chotto go-shohkigh shimas, …san des*
This is my wife	*Kore-wa tsuma des*
This is my daughter	*Kore-wa musumay des*
This is my mother	*Kore-wa haha des*
This is my friend	*Kore-wa tomodachi des*
This is my husband	*Kore-wa otto des*
This is my son	*Kore-wa musko des*
This is my father	*Kore-wa chichi des*

How do you do	*Hajime-mashtay, dohzo yoroshku*
Pleased to meet you	*Omay-ni kakaretay ureshee des*
Where are you from?	*Okuni-wa dochira des-ka*
I'm from the U.S.A.	*Amerika desu*

Where are you staying?	*Doko-ni otomari des-ka*
In a hotel	*Hoteru-ni*
With friends	*Tomodachi-no tokoro-ni*
With relatives	*Shinseki-no tokoro-ni*
Are you here on your own?	*Shtori-day koraremashta-ka*
I'm on my own	*Shtori des*
I'm with my family	*Kazoku-to kimashta*
I'm with a friend/friends	*Tomodachi-to kimashta*
Are you married?	*Kekkon shtay imas-ka*
I'm married	*Kekkon shtay imasu*
– single	*doku shin des*
– separated/divorced	*rikon shtay imas*
– a widow/widower	*miboh-jin/yamomay des*
I live with someone	*Koibito-to sunday imas*

GRAMMAR POINTERS

- When introducing yourself, say watashi wa (name) *des*, which means 'I am (name)."
- To use past tense, change the verb *–masu* to *–mashita*, that is, *kimasu* (come) becomes *kimashita*, or *ikimasu* (go) becomes *ikimashita* (went)
- *Kore wa...des* translates to This is...so it's used to mention the name of an object
- *...wa nan des ka* translates to What is..., and is used to ask the name of an object

Chapter 5 – Day 4: Travelling

Asking for directions

Excuse me, could I ask you something?	*Sumimasen-nga*
I've lost my way	*Michi-ni mayottay shimattan-des-nga*
Is there a(n)... around here?	*Kono hen-ni...ga arimas-ka*
Is this the way to...?	*Kono michi-wa...e ikimas-ka*
Could you point it out on the map?	*Kono chizu-de yubi-sashtay kuda-sigh*

Getting around by car

You need an international driver's license if you're a foreigner and you want to drive around Japan using a car. The speed limit in urban areas is around 40 kph and 80 to 100 kph on highways. The driver's seat is on the right side of the car so if you've gotten used to driving from the left seat, it might take time to become familiar with the driving orientation. Some road signs are also written only in Japanese and toll fees can be expensive.

How many kilometers to the next gas station, please?

Tsugi-no gasorin-sutando-maday

nankiro gurigh des-ka

I would like...liters of..., please	*...o...rittoru onegigh-shimas*
– super	*high-oku*

– leaded *yoo-en*

– unleaded *mu-en*

– diesel *dee-zeru*

– regular gasoline i

I would like...yen's worth of gas, please *...en bun dakay gasorin o-negigh-shimas*

Fill her up, please *Mantan o-negigh-shimas*

Could you check...? *...o tenken shitay kuda-sigh*

– the oil level *oyru*

– the tire pressure *tighya-no kooki-ats*

Could you change the oil, please? *Oyru-o ka-etay kuremas-ka*

Could you clean the windows/the windshield, please? *(fronto) Garas-o fu-itay kuremas-ka*

Could you wash the car, please? *Sensha o-negigh-shimas*

General

Where does this train *Kono densha-wa doko-e ikimas-ka*

go to?

Does this boat go to...? *Kono funay-wa...e ikimas-ka*

Can I take this bus to...? *Kono bas-wa...e ikimas-ka*

Does this train stop at...? *Kono densha-wa...ni tomarimas-ka*

Are these the priority seats?	*Kono seki-wa you-sen seki des-ka*
Is this seat free?	*Kono seki-wa ightay imas-ka*
– reserved?	*Kore-wa shtay-seki des-ka*
I've reserved...	*Yoyaku shimashta*
Could you tell me where I have to get off for...?	*...e iku-hgani-wa, doko-de oriru-ka oshi etay kuda-sigh*
Could you let me know when we get to...?	*...ni tsui-tara oshi-etay kuda-sigh*
Could you stop at the next stop, please?	*Tsugi-no bas-tay-de oroshtay kuda-sigh*
Where are we now?	*Ima dono-hen des-ka*
Do I have to get off here?	*Koko-de ori-nakereba-narimasen-ka*
Have we already passed...?	*...o tohri-mashta-ka*
How long have I been asleep?	*Watasi-wa dono gurigh nemuri mashta-ka*
How long does...stop here?	*...wa koko-ni dono-kurigh tomattay imas-ka*
I have Japan Rail Pass JR	*pas wo motte imas*

Can I come back on the same ticket?	*Kono kippu-wa ohf-ku des-ka*
Can I change on this ticket?	*Kono kippu-de norikae-raremas-ka*
How long is this ticket valid for?	*Kono kippu-wa itsu maday yookoh des-ka*

Customs

A passport is necessary for all visitors to Japan. Citizens of most European countries do not need a visa if they are staying as tourists up to 90 days. Visitors from the US, Canada, and New Zealand need a visa for visits of over 90 days. They are easily obtainable and free. Visitors from Australia need a visa for any visit. Drugs, firearms, and pornography may not be taken into Japan. Non-residents can take in duty-free 400 cigarettes, or 100 cigars, or 500g of tobacco; 3 bottles of alcohol (760cc each); 50g perfume; and other goods up to 200,000 yen in value. Personal possessions are exempt.

Trains

• The railway system in Japan is very well developed, and managed by Japan Railways (JR) and a large number of private railway companies. Intercity trains are local (futsoo), express (kyookoh), limited express (tokkyoo), and super express (shinkansen). Tickets are charged by distance, with surcharges for the category of train, class, and seat reservations. Ticket reservations are made at counters called "green windows" (midori no madoguchi). Tickets can be bought from ticket machines and most of these have an English option. The full fare does not have to be paid before the destination. Fare adjustment machines and counters are available. All JR stations show station names written in Japanese with the romanization below. Useful for travelers is the custom of including the names of the previous and next stations to the left and right underneath the station name.

Taxis

• Taxis are expensive, but all are metered and there is no custom of tipping. Carry the address and phone number of your destination, and a map of the immediate location if possible, to give to the driver. Taxi doors are automated; normally the back curbside door is the only one used. On arrival, wait for the driver to open the door, and do not close it yourself.

Taxi	*Tak-shee*
Could you get me a taxi, please?	*Tak-shee-o yonday kuda-sigh*
Where can I find a taxi around here?	*Tak-shee noriba-wa doko des-ka*
Could you take me to..., please?	...maday o-negigh shimas
– this address	kono joosho
– the...hotel	...hoteru
– the town/city center	choo-shin-chi
– the station	eki
– the airport	koo-koh
How much is the trip to...?	...maday ikura des-ka
How far is it to...?	...maday nan-kiro gurigh des-ka
I'm in a hurry	Iso-iday irun des-nga
Could you speed up/ slow down a little?	Motto hayaku/yukkuri ittay kuda-sigh

Could you take a different route?	Hoka-no michi-o tottay kuda-sigh
I'd like to get out here, please	Koko-de oroshtay kuda-sigh
You have to go straight on	...massugu ittay kuda-sigh
You have to turn left	...hidari-ni magattay kuda-sigh
You have to turn right	...migi-ni magattay kuda-sigh
This is it	Koko des
Could you wait a minute for me, please?	Chotto mattay-tay kuda-sigh

Chapter 6 – Day 5: Eating Out

Ordering

Waiter!	Wehtah-san!
Waitress!	Wehtres-san!
We'd like something to eat	Nani-ka tabe-tigh-n des-nga
We'd like a drink	Nani-ka nomi-tigh-n des-nga
Could I have a quick meal?	Nani-ka hayaku dekiru shina-wa arimas-ka
We'd like to have a drink first	Mazu nani-ka nomi-tig-n des-nga
Do you have a menu in English?	Aygo no menyoo-wa arimas-ka
Do you have a dish of the day?	Kyoh no menyoo-wa arimas-ka
We haven't made a choice yet	Mada kimarimasen
What do you recommend?	O-susume-hin-wa nan des-ka
What are the specials?	Tokubetsu ryohri-wa nan des-ka
I don't like...	...wa ski ja nigh-n des
I don't like fish	Sakana-wa ski ja nigh-n des
I don't like meat	Niku-wa ski ja nigh-n des
What's this?	Koray-wa nan des-ka
Does it have...in it?	...nga ha-ittay imas-ka
Is this sweet?	Kono ryohri-wa a-migh des-ka

Is this spicy?	Kono ryohri-wa ka-righ des-ka
Do you have anything else, please?	Hoka-ni nani-ka arimas-ka
I'm on a salt-free diet	Sheeo-nuki-de onegai-shimas
I can't eat pork	Butaniku-wa taberare-masen
Do you have a knife and fork?	Nighf to fohk arimas-ka
A little more rice please	Gohan moh skoshi onegigh-shimas
Another glass of water, please	Mizu moh ip-pigh onegigh-shimas
Do you have salt and pepper?	Sheeo to koshoh arimas-ka
Do you have a napkin?	Napukin arimas-ka
Do you have a spoon?	Spoon arimas-ka
Cheers!	Kam-pigh
Thank you for the meal.	Gochi soh sama deshta

Some of the most popular dishes in Japan

Sushi – Rice mixed with vegetables, cooked or raw fish, and other ingredients and then seasoned with vinegar. Probably the most famous Japanese dish.

Tonkatsu – Pork cutlets covered with breadcrumbs and then deep fried, served with a thick brown dipping sauce

Yakitori – Small chicken pieces, marinated and cooked barbecue style.

Yakisoba – Translates to 'fried noodles'. Uses small cuts of pork, ramen noodles, onions, cabbage, and carrots seasoned with a special yakisoba sauce.

Chapter 7 – Day 6: Shopping

Shops in Japan usually open at 10am and close at 8pm. Depending on the day, and the store itself, department stores close around 6 to 7pm. Small neighborhood shops are usually closed on Sundays while large malls are open all week long. There are 24 hour convenience stores around urban localities. Keep in mind that there's 5% sales tax on every item bought that the display price does not include.

Shopping conversations

Where can I get...?	...wa dono mise-ni arimas-ka
When does this shop open?	Kono mise-wa its akimas-ka
Could you help me, please? I'm looking for...	Sumimasen-nga,... ga hoshee-n des-nga
Could you tell me where the...department is?	...uriba-wa doko des-ka
Do you sell English newspapers?	Eigo-no shimbun-mo arimas-ka ...o kuda-sigh
I'm just looking	Chotto mite-iru dakay des
I'd also like...	...mo kuda-sigh
Could you show me...?	...o misetay kuda-sigh
Do you have something...?	...no-wa arimasen-ka
– less expensive?	motto ya-sui
– something smaller?	motto chee-sigh
– something larger?	motto oh-kee

I'll take this one	Koray kuda-sigh
Does it come with instructions?	Setsumaysho-wa hight-tay imas-ka
It's too expensive	Chotto taka-sugimas
Could you keep this for me? I'll come back for it later	Azukattay kudasa-i-masen-ka. Ato-de tori-ni kimas
Have you got a bag for me, please?	Bineeru bukuro arimas-ka
Could you gift wrap it, please?	Prezento des-kara, ts-tsunday kuda-sigh
I don't need a bag.	Fukuro wa die-job des.
Can I have a receipt?	Re-she-to wo morae maska.

Food

I'd like a hundred grams of..., please ...o hyaku gram o-negigh-shimas

– five hundred grams/ ... o gohyaku-gram

half a kilo of...

– a kilo of... ... o ichi-kiro

Could you...it for me, ... kuda-sigh

please?

Could you slice it/chop it for me, please?	Usuku/sigh-nomay-ni kittay kuda-sigh
Could you grate it for me, please?	Oroshtay kuda-sigh
Can I order it?	Choomon dekimas-ka
I'll pick it up tomorrow/at...	Ashta/... ji-ni tori-ni kimas
Can you eat this?	Tabemono des-ka
Can you drink this?	Nomimono des-ka
What's in it?	Zigh-ryoh-wa nan des-ka

Clothing and shoes

I'd like something to go with this	Nani-ka kore-ni ni-au-no-ga hoshee-n des-nga
Do you have shoes to match this?	Kore-ni ni-au kuts-ga arimas-ka
I'm a size...in the U.S.	Amerika no ... sighz nan des-nga
Can I try this on?	Shi-chaku dekimas-ka
Where's the fitting room?	Shi-chaku-shits-wa doko des-ka
It doesn't fit	Kono sighz-wa igh-masen
This is the right size	Kono sighz-wa digh-johbu des
It doesn't suit me	Ni-igh imasen
The heel's too high/low	Kakato-ga taka-sugimas/hiku-sugimas
Is this/are these genuine leather?	Kore-wa hontoh-no kawa des-ka
I'm looking for a...for a three-year-old child	San-sigh-no kodomo-no tame-ni ... ga hoshee-n des-nga
I'd like a silk...	Kinu-no...o-negigh shimas
– cotton...	Momen-no...o-negigh shimas
– woolen...	Wooru-no...o-negigh shimas
– linen...	Asa-no...o-negigh shimas
What temperature can I wash it at?	Sentaku ondo-wa nando des-ka
Will it shrink in the wash?	Arat-tara, chijimi-mas-ka

Chapter 8 – Day 7: Emergencies

Calling a doctor

Could you call/get a Doctor quickly, please?	Hayaku o-isha-san-o yonday/tsretay kitay kuda-sigh
When does the doctor have office hours?	O-isha-san-no shinsats-jikan-wa its des-ka
When can the doctor come?	O-isha-san-wa its koremas-ka
I'd like to make an appointment to see the doctor	O-isha-san-no yoyaku-o shtay kuda-sigh
I've got an appointment to see the doctor at...	Watashi-wa ... ji-ni o-isha-san-ni au yakusoku-ga arimas
Which doctor (druggist has night/weekend duty?	Dono isha (yak-kyoku)-ga yakin/ shoomats kimmu des-ka

What's wrong?

I don't feel well Gu-igh-ga waru-i-n des

I'm dizzy Me-migh-ga shimas

– ill Byohki des

– sick Kibun-ga waru-i-n des

I've got a cold Kazay des

It hurts here	Koko-ga i-tigh-n des
I’ve been throwing up	Modoshtay shimatta-n des
I’m running a temperature of...degrees	...do-no nets-ga arimas
I’ve been stung	...ni sasare-mashta
– by a hornet	suzume-bachi
– by an insect	mushi
– by a jellyfish	kuragay
I’ve been bitten	...ni kamare-mashta
– by a dog	inu
– by a snake	hebi
– by an animal	dohbuts
I’ve cut myself	Kiri-kizu-o tskemashta
I’ve burned myself	Yakedo-o shimashta

Asking for help

Help!	Tas-ketay!
Fire!	Kaji!
Police!	Kay-sats!
Quick!	Hayaku!
Danger!	Abu-nigh!
Watch out!/Be careful!	Abu-nigh!
Stop!	Tomaray!
Don’t!	Shi-nigh-de!/suru-na!

Let go!	Te-o doketay yo!/Te-o hanashtay!
Stop that thief!	Doroboh-o tometay!
Could you help me, please?	Tas-ketay kuda-sigh
Where's the police station/emergency exit /fire escape?	Kaysats-sho/hijoh-guchi/hinan-kigh dan-wa doko des-ka
Where's the fire extinguisher?	Shohkaki-wa doko-des-ka
Call the fire department!	Shohbohsha-o yonday!
Call the police!	Kaysats-o yonday!
Call an ambulance!	Kyookyoosha-o yonday!
Where's the nearest phone?	Denwa-wa doko des-ka
Could I use your phone?	Denwa-o ts-kawashtay kuda-sigh
What's the number for the police?	Kay-sats-wa namban des-ka

Lost items

I've lost my digital camera	Deji-kame-o naku-shimashta.
I've left my cell phone on the train	*Densha-ni kay-tigh wo wasurete shimai mashita.*
I've lost my purse/wallet	*Sighfu-o naku-shimashta*

I left my...yesterday *Kinoh...o okiwasure-mashta*

I left my...here *Koko-ni...o oki-wasure-mashta*

Did you find my...? *Watashi-no...ga mitsukari-mashta-ka*

It was right here *Koko-ni arimashta*

It's quite valuable *Totemo kichoh-hin des*

Where's the lost and found property office? *Wasuremono-kakari-wa doko des-ka*

Accidents

Robbery and violent crime are rare in Japan. The police maintain a visible presence through a network of small police stations called koban, usually found near railway stations. The police officers will help you find an address.

There's been an accident *Jiko-ga okimashta*

Someone's fallen into the water *Shto-ga mizu-ni ochimashta*

There's a fire *Kaji des*

Is anyone hurt? *Kega-o shita shto imas-ka*

Some people have been injured *Keganin-ga imas*

No one's been injured *Keganin-wa imasen*

There's someone in Shto-ga mada kuruma/ressha-ni

the car/train still nokottay imas

It's not too bad. Sore-hodo demo arimasen. Shimpigh

Don't worry shi-nigh-de kuda-sigh

Leave everything the way it is, please — Nani-mo sawara-nigh-de kuda-sigh

I want to talk to the police first — Mazu kaysats-to hanashi-tigh-n des

I want to take a photo first — Mazu shashin-o tori-tigh-n des

Here's my name and address — Kore-ga watashi-no na-migh-to joosho des

Could I have your name and address? — Anata-no na-migh-to joosho-o oshietay kuda-sigh

Could I see some identification/your insurance papers? — Mibun shohmaysho/hokan-shohsho-o misetay kuda-sigh

Will you act as a witness? Shohnin-ni nattay kuremas-ka

I need the details the insurance — Hoken-no tame-ni shoh-sigh-ga hits yoh des

Are you insured? — Hoken-ni hight-tay imas-ka

Could you sign here, please? — Koko-ni sign-o shtay kuda-sigh

Theft

I've been robbed — Nusu-mare-mashta

My...has been stolen — ...ga nusu-mare-ma

Chapter 9 – Where to Go From Here

Now that you have learned the basics of the Japanese language and have gotten more confident conversing with the local tongue, you may want to improve your vocabulary and conversational skills. You may also want to learn how to write Japanese using the hiragana and katakana approach. Here are some tips to get you on to the road of learning more about the rich Japanese culture.

1. Thanks to the proliferation and popularity of manga (Japanese comic books), anime (Japanese animated cartoons), and artsy Japanese movies, access to sample materials has never been easier. Learn how to pronounce Japanese words and structure sentences better by listening to the local tongue through multimedia. It's truly a fun way to learn more about this wonderful language.

2. Enroll in a Japanese writing class. Writing in hiragana or katakana is something that should not be done without supervision, preferably from a professional. It's all about the proper strokes and it won't be as wonderful if you just try to learn it by yourself.

3. Get advanced lessons in the Japanese language. There are a advanced classes available both online or your local language school. If you really want to dig deeper and be able to express yourself more clearly using the language, you should level up from the basics and get advances classes. The lessons might be quite a bit harder than the ones found on this book but it will be all worth it when you realize what you can learn from these classes.

4. Invest in quality material. There are books, both printed and digital, and there are applications that can give you further lessons on the Japanese language.

Read the reviews and buy those you think can help you learn more about the Japanese language.

5. Practice. Follow the lyrics of a Japanese song. You may start with Japanese nursery rhymes and work your way to mainstream songs. Karaoke sessions with the locals are an excellent way of making new friends as well as advancing your Japanese language skills. Use the language as often as possible to familiarize yourself until speaking it becomes second nature.

6. Have a conversation buddy. He doesn't have to be a Japanese language tutor. He can be someone who also wants to learn English which makes it a great opportunity for both of you to teach each other. There's no better way to learn another language than with someone who speaks it as native tongue.

7. Immerse yourself into the country and the culture. That way you not only learn how to speak advanced Japanese but also learn more about the country. There are also community immersion programs available locally that should give you a good start if you're not going to Japan in the near future.

PS: Can I Ask You A Quick Favor?

If you liked the book, please leave a nice review on Amazon! I´d absolutely love to hear your feedback. Every time I read your reviews… you make me smile. I´d be immensely thankful if you go to Amazon now and write down a quick line sharing with me your experience. I personally read ALL the reviews there, and I´m thrilled to hear your feedback and honest motivation. It´s what keeps me going, and helps me improve everyday =)

Please go Amazon Now and Drop A quick review sharing your experience !

***

THANKS!

***

ONCE YOU´RE BACK,FLIP THE PAGE!

BONUS CHAPTER AHEAD

=)

About the Author

Hitomi Nakamura was born on May 11 in Yokohama, Japan. Her parents raised her in accordance with Japanese culture, and she spent much of her childhood cooking traditional Japanese meals with her mother and celebrating the country's most cherished holidays.

Academically, she excelled in the Japanese language and writing, which eventually led her to pursue her gift of words professionally. Today, she's committed to sharing her love of literature and Japanese culture with as many people as possible. By teaching others her native tongue and customs, she hopes to keep alive the beauty, uniqueness, and history of Japan.